Thomas M. Disch

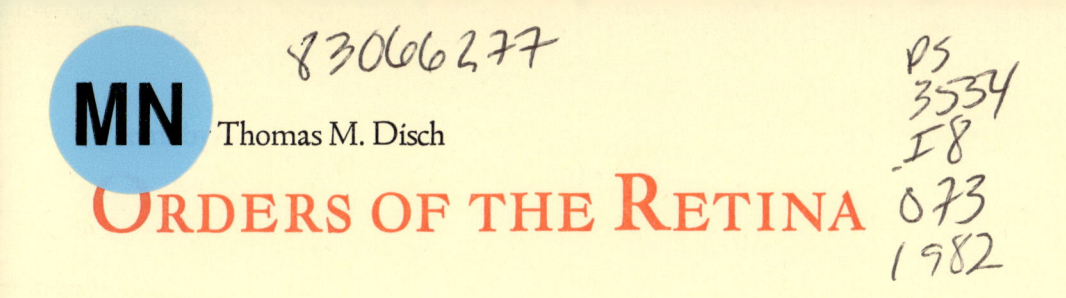

ORDERS OF THE RETINA

The Toothpaste Press : West Branch, Iowa : April 1982

Acknowledgements

Some of these poems have appeared in Contact II, The Little Magazine, New Worlds, Open Places, Pandora, Partisan Review, Penumbra, Prairie Schooner, Times Literary Supplement, Toothpaste & Transatlantic Review.

"The Prisoners of War" & "Luxe, Calme et Desespoir" first appeared in Poetry (Chicago).

© 1982 by Thomas M. Disch

The publishers wish to thank the National Endowment for the Arts and the Iowa State Arts Council for a Small Press Assistance Grant.

Library of Congress CIP Data

Disch, Thomas M.
   Orders of the retina.

   I. Title.
PS3554.I807   811'.54   82-4728
ISBN 0-915124-60-2 (signed)   AACR2
ISBN 0-915124-61-0 (pbk.)

Contents

9 The Goldberg Variations
10 Anniversary Valentine
11 Litany
12 Pronouns
13 Delete 'Stars'
14 The First Cuckoo
15 Causes and Effects
16 The Childhood of Language
17 Invictus
18 To the Sun
19 To a Tree
20 Three Boxes
21 Hands and Mouth
22 Luxe, Calme et Desespoir
23 What It Was Like
24 Listening to the News
25 In the Picture
26 Turner Jigsaw
27 After Ostade
28 The New Fashions
29 The Madness of Uniforms,
   The Sadness of Laundromats
30 Come, Pleasant Death
31 Le Tombeau de Bach (Richard)
32 The Prisoners of War
33 Light Verses for the Viet Nam Dead
34 Epistle

35 Bourgeois Idyll
36 Coming of Age
37 The Decaying Swan
38 The First Christmas Tree
39 Stars as Thought
40 No Form, No Content
41 Erosion
42 Painting 1/8/80
43 Painting 1/11/80
44 Painting 1/13/80
45 What to Accept

for Ronald, Leonard, Cyril, Dick, and Mother

The Goldberg Variations

When suddenly a tricycle got up
with Christmas bells started bouncing down
the stairs, and then with just a tremor
of hesitation (think of the too-strenuous
handshake of an aging banker) turned
round the corner, to encounter its own
image; so might a child in a hospital
bed, leafing through old magazines,
come upon a photo of his own face
in some ad for an obscure charity—
without astonishment, without feeling sad.

Anniversary Valentine

We may not know what we feel—
Whether a touch is the real
Pressure of hands on a heart,
Or if it is only art—

But that needn't give us pause.
Without unambiguous laws
Cities would go up in flames.
Let us kiss, and state our aims.

Litany

Sender of blue days & blissful silences
Sponsor of dreams
Theorem of a Grand Bahama
Thumbprint of the soul
Source of all stories & their final draft
Four-color separation of the unattainable Ideal
Idol before whom all idols else must bow
Fountain of the waterglass
Believer of all things unbelievable
Incredible giraffe
          Misere nobis

Smiling pavement of a perfect street
Prince of lost shoes
Supreme graffito in the washroom of the world
Laughter of midnight telephones
Voice & velocity of light
Unwitnessable glade
Whiteness within the lie
Sweet beribboned lamb of stone
Alarmclock of eternity
Doctrine most dear
          Ora pro nobis

Pronouns

Why do I resent *them* so?
Their silly posturing,
Their catalogues of this and that,
Their endless discussions of her,
Their diatribes against him—
All of it quite boring,
But they don't mean it
As an affront to *me*.
It's just the way they are.

Ah, why trouble *you*
With all this? You are as mute
And mysterious as ever. Who
Could help loving you?

You don't reply.

It is a lonely life,
Living as I do—
For I alone, of all the pronouns,
Am always myself, always true.

Ah, darling, let us leave them—
Let us go away, just you and I,
To somewhere free
Of all limiting reference
Where we can be simply ourselves.

Delete 'Stars'

As you listen, on your modest balcony,
To the party in the penthouse overhead:

As the guard's flashlight sweeps
The walls, and single window, of your cell:

As you waltz beneath the interlacing tiers
Of cloverleaf ramps:

As you kneel with your taper and pray
To the bearded faces on the tesseraed dome:

As you leap from the trench screaming
"France and my bayonet!":

As you soar up from the bleachers
Electrified by a song:

As your past appears, naked and irradiated,
In a vision of Judgement:

The lights in the sky are,
Respectively,

Cigars,
      bars,
           cars,
                czars,
Gloire's,
      guitars,
           & scars.

The First Cuckoo

At six o'clock and, still, at half past six
The light lies roseate upon the bricks
That overlook the Midtown Parking Lot.
It's more than warm, it's very nearly hot.
In short-sleeved shirts the proudest torsos strut
(Though some, alas, have rather gone to gut);
The joggers jog, for joy, an extra mile,
And even derelicts are seen to smile.
Resounding with the rediscovered song
Of motorcycles pent all winter long
In cellar tombs, the streets are suddenly alive
With the gladsome buzzing of the urban hive.
    Rejoice, you millions! Fill the streets with flesh:
    Our death is dead, and life's alive and fresh.

Causes and Effects

for Harry Harrison

A special cam that rides the curve
That takes its pattern from the nerve
That fires when a certain star
Is visible above the bar
That hypothetically unites
Opposing helices of lights
That blink and glimmer on the cue
Of what is thought of what we do
By maidens dancing in a ring
Has moved—and suddenly it's spring.

The Childhood of Language

for Chip and Iva

The tree isn't here, and I am
Not asleep. Sometimes there are
Children in the tree. Sometimes
He takes me out into the other room
Before the grown-ups have left.
Sometimes he holds me up
And I can touch the ceiling.
Tomorrow when he takes me to the park
I will say the right word,
I will say 'tree' and maybe he will untie
My shoes and let me walk upside-down
On the blue ceiling of the tree,
And all the grown-ups will have to watch
Me, the wonderful baby.

Invictus

Body, Body, bring my mind
To somewhere only you can find,
Somewhere so dark that touch alone
Can trace its way from bone to bone,
Somewhere immense and overgrown,
A place where granite millwheels grind
Acres of grain on a mammoth stone.

Body, Body, carry me
Above the roofs my eyes can see
Into prismatic realms of light
Where time is shorn of day and night
And thought becomes an endless flight
Through spiralling eternity
Upon the flesh's paper kite.

To the Sun

      Shine, Sun, that I may see
The flecks my retina most freely makes
      Association to. Give it cause
For reflection. Decorate the diorama
Of the world you're not yourself a part of
      With your old claim that you alone
      Are sole source of all energies
Whatsoever. Let it please us to know
      Your light, however shattered
Into chandeliers and oil fields, is all
The light there is. Prove to me, Immensity,
      That I, too, am my own universe—
      And not, at the same time:
Being begot, as you, out of a kind
      Of solipsistic slime, a stew
Of imponderable depth and beauty.
      Only Sun, it's you I adore—
And me I'll have no other sun before.

To a Tree

Doff, O doff those shabby rags
   That so gallantly you wore
When first you got into my bed.
   Take them off and nevermore
Put them on again. Instead

Wrap your pretty limbs in these
   Flags of blue and white and red:
They are fires in the breeze
   Of common sense and flutter
In your hair, like hummingbirds.

How I adore you when you wear,
   Ornamental as despair,
Nests as empty as the words
   Of poets when in jest they utter
Intimations of unease.

Three Boxes

In one of them
Some hands
Dance
In dry sand

Another is filled
With the wet
Thumps
Of the heart

The third serenely
Thinks
Of peach
Colored curls

Spilling over
The beach
The sun
Sinks

A garbage man
Gathers
The hearts
And hands.

Hands and Mouth

Obedient as bombardiers, the ruthless hands
Cover the protesting mouth, deaf
To its reasons. They have always known
Themselves to be, at last, the more
Intelligent. Imagine a mouth
Playing a piano! Or plastering!
No more food, mouth: those are
Orders. Just shut your trap.
If you have something to say, we
Will help you write it.

Mouth exposes a row of chipped enamel
Tiles and hums like an icebox
The hymn of its maddening desires.
For a little while the hands cling
To the mast. Then with a vast slurp
They slide down the long funnel
Into the contented belly of the sea.
Long afterwards a bottle appears at the foot
Of the bed filled with cryptic messages:
We are happy. Come and rescue us. Beware.

Luxe, Calme, et Desespoir

Pipe and bottle both are there—
A plate, a knife, some Camembert;
One window frames the evening air,
Opaquely brown as earthenware.
Observe the woman in the chair—
The limp disorder of her hair,
The way her dull eyes seem to stare
Beyond the picture plane to where
The viewer feigns a bland despair.

What It Was Like

Like a wine that burns the tongue
And leaves it thirstier, like glimpses
Into lit interiors from the windows
Of slow-moving trains, like rain
On pavements when the sky is clear,
Like isolated lines of verse
Reverberating in the mind,
Like figures in disturbing dreams
Condensed by waking to an article
Of clothes, like the loud cries
Of frogs or insects in the night
Or like the golden light of sundogs
Through a rift of cloud, like memories
Of wordless lies, like flies that buzz
About an opened fruit, like clothing
Folded in a drawer or like a pain
That vanishes as soon as felt,
Like butter melting in a bowl
Or like the color of a shoal of sand
As waves wash over it, like salamanders
Scurrying from walls, like postcards
Of suburban shopping malls,
Like scores of games with pencilled names
Of friends forgotten long ago or like
A song dissolving in an empty room
While in the street below imported saplings
Glitter in the passing lights of cars.

Listening to the News

Loud music and thick doors

Yesterday's breakdown becomes
the anecdote for dinner tonight

I reach forward to adjust the knobs
of your dress   I am all ears

& it is ringing again

Such a sensation when
breath becomes the boat sailing in

Archipelagoes that have evolved
uncatalogued species of finch

In the garden I grew insane

Meanwhile the mailman grows bored
sitting for his portrait

He asks me how do I pronounce my name
I tell him I don't know

The light is lovely in the south of France

In the Picture

Not a rabbit
but a darkness
with that shape

It seems unable to participate
in the easy solidarity
of lemons and leaves

Even more is it at odds
with these butcher-shop sections
of crimson flesh

Yet it is not without
a sense of conveying
some very definite meaning

The eye keeps coming back to it
as we return to the decaying neighborhood
we lived in and managed to leave

They were not our lives we were living then
but someone else's, whose address,
thankfully, is forgotten

There he remains
unvisitable and demented
a figure in a window high above the street

Turner Jigsaw

The sea's complete, the sky is all to do—
Except the portion over to the right
Where sunlight pierces the clouds to pure flake white,
Transmutes a yielding oyster-greyness to
A faltering and then a limpid blue.
Now to sort out varieties of light:
Some featureless and some with malachite
Marblings; some bright, some dull; all but a few,
However, like as homonyms, of a hue
That can't be called grey and isn't quite
A blue. Since color offers so little clue,
It might make sense to go by shape. This bite
Must have a knob that it attaches to,
Which yearns, as stalagmite to stalactite,
Towards some other missing knob. I knew
I never should have started this. I'm through:
As much is done as I will ever do.
Back in the box! Good riddance and good night.

After Ostade

The drunkard totters gaily on the brink
Of his permitted, so-far-safe despair,
While down the road a derelict, whose hair
Is parted by a wound, gives him a wink,
As who would say, we *both* could use a drink.

The New Fashions

The moment you give up
precedes
the moment you know what you've done

The hand relaxes.

& when it tries
to raise the weights again
there's no strength left—
not in the fingers,

not in the arms,
not in the small of the back.

Your smile grows brighter.
Your wit's admired by the other guests.

"Ravishing!"
"Inspired!"
"Is it gold lamé?"

The Madness of Uniforms,
The Sadness of Laundromats

The boots flirt with a confidence the dun shirt
Denies. The jacket would like to be thought
Smart, but the tie whispers of hours enslaved
To calamity. Can any poet ever absolutely leap
Free of his origins? Can the tongue name its desire?

The socks that have been left behind
Hang from the chrome hook of the bleach dispenser
Mute and futureless: one brown, one black,
One blue. So many poets who are dead!
Whose books will never be opened again!

Come, Pleasant Death

Come, pleasant Death, and decorate my tomb
   With lush, banal decalcomania!
   Sink me as you sank the Lusitania!
Enshroud me with your deep Miltonic gloom!
Come, dressed in leather, blacker than the night
   The power failed and all the lights went out.
   Come, ravish me, and let me no more doubt
Your boots can trample and your teeth can bite.
—Like this! Your belly slack and tattoos dim?
Your arches fallen and a double chin?
   A *plastic* handle on your riding crop?
   When *was* the last time you were at a gym?
I really wonder that they let you in.
   Dear Death, do let's just let the matter drop.

Le Tombeau de Bach (Richard)

He lacks, like every aeronaut, the means
Of love. Him here, it there—they don't embrace.
The emblematic clouds, a sky's machines
For teaching him the elements of space
And time, withhold their gifts of rain and grace,
Announce a quiz. He groans. Assorted greens
He must identify are flashed on the screens
Of the deep. The first is False. He cannot place
The next, and guesses All of the Above.
The moon's immense counter-hypothesis
Looms in the east, one thought beyond his reach.
The slides repeat, and none of them is Love.
He dives into the sky's synoptic kiss,
And learns at last the lesson it can teach.

The Prisoners of War

Their language disappeared a year or so
after the landscape: so what can they do now
but point? At parts of bodies, at what
they want to eat, at instrument panels, at
new highways and other areas of intense
reconstruction, at our own children smiling
into cameras, at the lettering on cannisters,
at streaks of green and purple, at the moon,
at moments that may still suggest such concepts
as "Civilization" or "Justice" or "Terror,"
and at ourselves, those still alive, who stand
before what might have been, a year ago, a door.

Light Verses for the Viet Nam Dead

The mole in its hole and the cat in its bag
Know what no rossignol ever will know:
The peace of final placement, as when a flag
Arrives at Arlington, and flies, and witnesses, below,
The pure rectangularity of the buried nation,
The tribute of the lawn, the triumph and the tribulation
Of the serried names, rank on rank, each name
At last where it must belong, and all aflame
With a common fame and a single shame and one lie
In every throat, and in every socket of every eye
A tear that is just the same, and the flag as it waves
Above the graves expresses to the wind, as it passes
And ruffles the stars and the stripes, and stirs the grasses,
The wish forever unexpressed by the men within their graves—
That the wind should erase and leave no trace
Of the letters on every stone, the smile on every face.

Epistle

Leave your tribe
The women in your tribe are old
Your goats are thin

Join my tribe
In my tribe we have long holidays
There is lots of room

Leave your tribe
Already the government troops approach
To fire your dwellings

Join my tribe
For we have been allowed to live
In this valley for all time

Bourgeois Idyll

Roses and candles with the dinner speak
Of the wine's fulfilled wish,
Of the wisdom of painters choosing
To paint in available light
As it swings a shadow
Around the curves of
Vase and petal. The flame travels
Down to its root in the brass
Candlestick. The empty bottle
Springs out of existence
Down the mysterious
Incinerator. Now is the hour of tv
And the proper positioning of cushions.
News is related, goods are sold,
And the channel changes to 13.
Suddenly our Seurat
Is a Matisse. Bright are the lamps
And warm the tone of orange
Flowering in the upholstery.
Julia Child has cooked another perfect meal.
The dishes can wait till morning.

Coming of Age

Here's the treason he didn't foresee:
Not a willing rush to the main advantage
The way that Jack instantly succumbed
To his wife's father's wherewithal;
Not even the grudging surrender
Of fresh tar to the feet of midtown pedestrians
As when Alice finally stopped trying
To dance; not the petulant despair
Of Max, stoking his emphysema
With forty Camels a day; nor Evan's defections
From the successive governments
Of his three wives—none of these.
Simply the depletion of reserves,
The discovery on the coldest night of the year
That there isn't any fuel for the furnace,
The disappearance of a smile still bright at 3 a.m.

The Decaying Swan

The hymn by which the swan proclaims its death—
To whom is it addressed? It is a bait to tempt
The taps of cans and tips of lances down
To the altars of a buried temple where,
Illumined by its songs, a lurid pool
Forms on the floor of the fane. An oil station's
Walls would be cleaner: look at the tarry scum
That coats the basin of the font, those rotting fruits
Heaped up before the tiny dove-drawn hearse.
Hearken to the faint, effective sound
That has relinquished resonance and dies
Without an echo's cadenced silences.
Obey it: take these consecrated flowers
From its mouth, and from its lichened eyes
These pallid sweets. Eat them—and be mortal.

Santa Claus saw her,
Fell in love, gave chase. She called
To her father, "Help!"

Stars as Thought

The sinking inward
of each tiny point
into a tinier

& forgetting
how it began

No Form, No Content

Off on my own
two days AWOL
      from my life
  & all I want to do
     is hole up
with a bottle of vin plonk

Writing
  or reading
      something riveting

Somewhere as quiet
    as this pub
  where I'm the only customer
    So lazy
    No feeling
A whole afternoon completely
     out of focus

    Alone
    in ancient China

        3.16.78
        The Pineapple

Erosion

God it feels good
Sometimes
        in this world
        of Yours
The years slip by:

        I grow old
You're there   I'm here
      Even the rain
        seems bent
        on cooperation

Painting 1/8/80

As when on entering the museum
Of a provincial town
One sees a painting known
From a thumbtacked postcard
And thinks, "Oh, that's here!"
So now, as these stones dance in a wall
Around my lyre, I feel a like
Consoling certainty—that deep
In the rural backwater of my own
Brushstrokes I shall hear, eternalized,
The twanging wires of the tango stretched
Between the uneroded marble of the mind
And the enchanted instant's fingertips.

PAINTING 1/11/80

We see here the beholder's
Reflective eye,
With beauty in it.

We see the retina reach out
To order the concentric air
In bands of color, and how

Each orifice receives
The vital message that comes
Simultaneously from the blue.

Painting 1/13/80

Report immediately, human,
To the golden age of faith.
Surrender your name at the door.

In the stony twilight within
Light a candle to the saint
In charge of the sun and growing vegetables.

Harrow the earth you own and adore.
Accept this weariness as proof
That you have lived in Arcady.

What to Accept

The fact of mountains. The actuality
Of any stone—by kicking, if necessary.
The need to ignore stupid people,
While restraining one's natural impulse
To murder them. The change from your dollar,
Be it no more than a penny,
For without a pretense of universal penury
There can be no honor between rich and poor.
Love, unconditionally, or until proven false.
The inevitability of cancer and/or
Heart disease. The dialogue as written,
Once you've taken the role. Failure,
Gracefully. Any hospitality
You're willing to return. The air
Each city offers you to breathe.
The latest hit. Assistance.
All accidents. The end.

Colophon

Handset by David Duer in Italian Olde Style type. Designed & printed by Allan Kornblum. The Curtis Tweedweave text was printed on an ATF Little Giant, (thanks to Tim Showalter for repairing the press fountain within four hours of a desperate call). 1,050 copies were Smyth sewn and glued into Strathmore Americana wrappers by Rebecca Henderson at Prairie Fox. 100 copies were numbered & signed by the author; quarter bound in cloth and Japanese stencil-dyed paper by Constance Sayre at Black Oak Bindery.

NORMANDALE COMMUNITY COLLEGE
LIBRARY
9700 FRANCE AVENUE SOUTH
BLOOMINGTON, MN 55431-4399